W9-AET-965

VICTOR CRUZ

Joanne Mattern

Mitchell Lane

PUBLISHERS
P.O. Box 196
Hockessin, Delaware 19707
Visit us on the web: www.mitchelllane.com
Comments? Email us: mitchelllane@mitchelllane.com

Mitchell Lane
PUBLISHERS

Printing   1   2   3   4   5   6   7   8   9

A Robbie Reader Biography

Abigail Breslin	Drake Bell & Josh Peck	Miguel Cabrera
Adrian Peterson	Dr. Seuss	Miley Cyrus
Albert Einstein	Dwayne "The Rock"	Miranda Cosgrove
Albert Pujols	Johnson	Philo Farnsworth
Aly and AJ	Dwyane Wade	Raven-Symoné
Andrew Luck	Dylan & Cole Sprouse	Robert Griffin III
AnnaSophia Robb	Emily Osment	Roy Halladay
Ashley Tisdale	Hilary Duff	Shaquille O'Neal
Brenda Song	Jamie Lynn Spears	Story of Harley-Davidson
Brittany Murphy	Jennette McCurdy	Sue Bird
Buster Posey	Jesse McCartney	Syd Hoff
Charles Schulz	Jimmie Johnson	Tiki Barber
Chris Johnson	Joe Flacco	Tim Lincecum
Cliff Lee	Jonas Brothers	Tom Brady
Dale Earnhardt Jr.	Keke Palmer	Tony Hawk
David Archuleta	Larry Fitzgerald	Troy Polamalu
Demi Lovato	LeBron James	**Victor Cruz**
Donovan McNabb	Mia Hamm	Victoria Justice

Library of Congress Cataloging-in-Publication Data
Mattern, Joanne, 1963–
Victor Cruz / by Joanne Mattern.
    pages cm. – (A Robbie reader)
Includes bibliographical references and index.
ISBN 978-1-61228-461-3 (library bound)
1. Cruz, Victor, 1983– –Juvenile literature. 2. Football players–United States–Biography–Juvenile literature. I. Title.
GV939.C783M38 2014
796.332092–dc23
[B]
                                                       2013023064
eBook ISBN: 9781612285191

ABOUT THE AUTHOR: Joanne Mattern is the author of more than 200 nonfiction books for young readers. Her books for Mitchell Lane include biographies of such notables as *Michelle Obama, Benny Goodman, Selena, LeBron James,* and *Peyton Manning.* Mattern lives in New York State with her husband, four children, and an assortment of pets.

TABLE OF CONTENTS

Words in **bold** type can be found in the glossary.

Victor Cruz is a hometown boy at heart. In 2012, he returned to Paterson, New Jersey, where he grew up, to sign copies of his new autobiography, *Out of the Blue.*

A Big Decision

Victor Cruz was alone and lost. He had been a star football player in high school. He had escaped the rough neighborhood of Paterson, New Jersey, and he had a chance at a college education and a life as a **professional** football player. Then he had thrown it all away. Cruz failed out of college. He lost his football **scholarship**. Now, the 20-year-old was working at a mall and going to **community college**. The only NFL football he saw was on television.

Cruz joined some friends for a night of partying. They were at a club when a fight broke out. Cruz heard gunshots. He quickly ran outside, sat on the curb, and started to think. He was tired of the life he was living. It was time for a change. "I decided that I was going to ace my final exams, get back into school, and achieve all of my goals," he later wrote in his autobiography, *Out of the Blue.* "No more

Cruz is a fan favorite. He shares a joyous moment with Giants fans after defeating the Green Bay Packers in January 2012.

excuses. No more pitying myself. No more sleepless nights spent staring at the ceiling. . . . No one was going to do it for me. No one was going to *give* me anything."

For the first time in months, Cruz felt excited. He realized he could accomplish anything he wanted to, if he just set his mind to it. When his friends ran up behind him, Cruz did not want to hear their story of what they'd seen in the club. "I'm done," he told them. "I'm going home."

Cruz put everything he had into his college classes. "I approached the next few months . . . like I would a big football game," he wrote. Cruz's hard work paid off. He finished the school year with four As and one B. Cruz's life was back on track. But even he didn't know that just a few years later, he would be one of the biggest stars in the NFL.

Cruz's mother, Blanca, has always supported her son and pushed him to do his best. He was proud to appear with her at a 2013 event honoring mothers.

Jersey Boy

Victor Michael Cruz was born on November 11, 1986, in Paterson, New Jersey. Victor's mother, Blanca Cruz, had moved to the United States from Puerto Rico when she was nine years old. She worked several jobs to support Victor and his younger sister, Andrea. Victor's father, Michael Walker, was an African-American firefighter who also had two other children, Ebony and Malik. Victor's mother raised him alone at first, but his father later became a big part of his life.

Victor and his mother lived with her parents in an apartment in Paterson. There was a lot of crime in their neighborhood. Victor loved sports and spent many hours playing in the streets and parks with his friends. However, he always had to be home for dinner at five o'clock sharp. One day he stayed out after five o'clock and was horrified when his grandmother came outside in a nightgown and slippers to find him. "I'd kick and scream about how unfair it was that all my friends were able to stay out playing sports until all hours of the night, but . . . they knew that if I was in the house by five, at that dinner table, I couldn't be somewhere else getting into trouble," Victor later wrote in his autobiography.

The Cruz family's apartment was above a martial arts studio. Victor started taking tae kwon do classes there when he was seven years old. He loved the discipline and focus he found there. Victor became a black belt when he was twelve years old. His teacher told him he was the youngest tae kwon do black belt in New Jersey history. Victor also enjoyed playing basketball with his friends and later played for several school teams.

Victor's father enjoyed watching football, and soon Victor was watching too. Even though the New York Giants played nearby, Victor was a Dallas Cowboys fan. The Cowboys were the best team in the NFL at that time. In the 1990s, they won three Super Bowls.

When Victor was 12 years old, he joined his first football team. He played with the PAL North Firefighters. The team was made up of the sons and nephews of local firefighters. Victor played **center**. But his father thought he should be a **running back**. Finally, the coach agreed and put Victor at that position during a game. Victor surprised everyone by carrying the ball 64 yards to score a touchdown. He never played center again!

Cruz's poor grades kept him out of college ball at first, but by 2008 he was a starter on the team at the University of Massachusetts. Wearing number 3, Cruz catches a pass during the first quarter of an NCAA game that October.

Struggles in School

Cruz started high school at a local technical school, but he really wanted to attend Paterson Catholic High School. The school was known for its athletic programs. Several top college and professional athletes had graduated from Paterson Catholic. Cruz transferred there in tenth grade. The school would give Cruz an excellent education and prepare him for college.

Cruz was a star on the basketball court and the football field. During his senior year in 2003, he earned All-State honors for football. Cruz caught 42 passes and scored 19 touchdowns that year. To top it off, the Cougars won a state championship.

Cruz decided to attend the University of Massachusetts and play on their football team. Colleges and universities cannot accept every student that applies, though. In order to decide which students they will accept, they consider a student's grades, activities, and scores on standard tests like the SAT. Cruz did not score well on the SAT. Without a good score, Cruz could not go to the University of Massachusetts. Instead, he went to Bridgton Academy in Maine, which was in a rural location very different from the city of Paterson. Even though it was hard to get used to this new environment, Cruz was able to focus on football and studying. His hard work paid off. Cruz took the SAT again and did well. He enrolled at the University of Massachusetts in the spring of 2005.

Unfortunately, once Cruz was there, he did not take college very seriously. His grades were so poor that he was asked to leave school.

When he returned in the fall of 2006, the same thing happened again. Cruz and his mother were horrified. Pamela Marsh-Williams helped run the advising department at the University of Massachusetts. She remembered how Blanca Cruz drove up to the school to beg them to let Cruz stay. "She said there was nothing waiting for Victor back home," Marsh-Williams told *The New York Times* a few years later. "UMass was supposed to be his gateway out of a tough neighborhood, and she feared for what would happen if he went back. She worried he would never get out."

It seemed like Blanca's fears would come true. "I was going to be another inner-city kid working at . . . some mall," Cruz told *The New York Times.* "I could have been there the rest of my life."

Cruz quickly became an important part of the New York Giants. In this game against the Dallas Cowboys in 2012, Victor does what he does best—catch a pass!

Getting Noticed

In March 2007, Cruz got the news that his father had died suddenly. He was crushed by his father's death. "My father was my idol," he wrote in his autobiography. "I think about him every time I step on the football field. . . . I think about him all the time." Today, Cruz runs to the end zone before every game. Then "I say a prayer and I talk to my father," he told *The New York Times.* "I have a conversation with him for a moment because I feel he's there and I want him to know that."

Cruz attended a community college to take the courses he needed to go back to UMass. He was successful. In 2007, Cruz enrolled at UMass for the third time. This time, his grades were good enough to play football. Sports reporter Rachel Nichols summed up Cruz's determination to make his dreams come true. "Most kids would've just said, 'Eh, this isn't for me.' Instead, Cruz said, 'I'm not good at this, but I need to figure out how to do it because I want to play football.'"

Cruz's first college game was in October 2007. He made the starting lineup for the team

Cruz doesn't let anything stop him on the football field. Here he stiff-arms New York Jets player Dwight Lowery to get past him during a preseason game in the summer of 2010.

in 2008, his junior year. Cruz was on fire. He led the team with 71 pass **receptions** for a total of 1,064 yards and six touchdowns. His senior year was almost as good. Cruz caught 59 passes for 868 yards and five touchdowns. Cruz was named to the CAA All-**Conference** First Team in both his junior and senior years.

In spite of his great numbers on the field, the NFL did not seem very interested in Cruz. He was not chosen in the 2010 NFL **draft**. Cruz was disappointed but he did not give up. After the draft, his agent called to tell him that the New York Giants had asked him to come to their training camp. But the coaches weren't sure about putting him on the team yet. They knew his college history and feared he might not be a good fit for their team.

Cruz was eager for a chance to prove himself. He loved the idea of playing for a team that was near his hometown. Cruz listened to everything the coaches told him, and began to play even better. In August 2010, Cruz became a wide **receiver** with the New York Giants.

Cruz couldn't contain his joy when the Giants won the Super Bowl on February 5, 2012. "I screamed like a little kid on Christmas," he wrote.

The Heart of a Champion

Cruz's 2010 season was cut short when he was injured in October. But early in the 2011 season, he began to show what he could do. He was catching multiple passes in each game, often totaling over 100 yards. Fans began to yell when Cruz was on the field. At first, he thought they were booing him. Instead, they were calling his name: "Cruuuz!" They loved how Cruz celebrated every touchdown with a **salsa** dance in honor of his grandmother. He says she taught him how to dance as a child.

The Giants made it into the **playoffs** and then the NFC Championship game against the

San Francisco 49ers. The 49ers could not hold Cruz back. He caught 10 passes for 142 yards. The Giants won 20-17. They were going to the Super Bowl!

The Giants faced the New England Patriots in the Super Bowl. New England was a

Cruz is almost as famous for his salsa dancing as he is for his football skills. He shared some salsa moves with fans during a Modell's store appearance in New York City in January 2012.

powerful team and many people thought they would win. Cruz scored the first touchdown of the game to give the Giants a 9-0 lead. But the Patriots came back slowly. With less than four minutes left in the game, the Giants were losing 17-15. The Giants had one final

Cruz was a big part of the Giants' Super Bowl win in February 2012. Here he catches a pass during the first half of the game.

chance. Quarterback Eli Manning led the team on a drive straight down the field. The Giants won 21-17. "I screamed like a little kid on Christmas," Cruz shared in his autobiography.

The Giants had a winning season in 2012–13, but did not make the playoffs. Then Cruz touched hearts all over the world after the tragic school shooting in Newtown,

People everywhere were moved by Cruz's tribute to Newtown shooting victim Jack Pinto. One of Jack's friends joined Newtown families at a Giants game two weeks after the shooting.

Connecticut, in December 2012. Cruz found out that one of the victims, six-year-old Jack Pinto, was a huge fan of his. Cruz honored the little boy during a game against the Atlanta Falcons. He wrote Pinto's name on his gloves and shoes during the game, along with the words "My Hero," and "This one is 4 u!" A few days later, Cruz visited the Pinto family

Cruz loves to show off his little girl! His daughter Kennedy was born in 2012.

Cruz often appears in public with his long-time girlfriend, Elaina Watley. She is from New Jersey, just like he is.

and gave his gloves and shoes to Jack's older brother Ben. "It was very emotional," Cruz later told *Newsday.* "It shows you how much of an effect you have on kids. . . . It really showed me how real it is to be a role model."

Cruz plans to continue playing football and being a role model for young people. He wants to help others who face challenges to achieve their goals. Today Cruz lives with his girlfriend, Elaina Watley, and their young daughter, Kennedy. He wants to show his daughter and all his fans that hard work is what counts. "You can't wait for your chance," he wrote in his autobiography. "You can't expect it. You have to earn it."

CHRONOLOGY

1986   Victor Cruz is born on November 11.

1999   Plays football in a local league.

2001   Enrolls at Paterson Catholic High School.

2003   Helps Paterson Catholic win the New Jersey parochial Group I championship; earns All-State honors.

2004   Graduates from Paterson Catholic; enrolls at Bridgton Academy in Maine.

2005   Enrolls at the University of Massachusetts on a football scholarship but is sent home because of poor grades.

2006   Returns to UMass but is once again forced to leave and loses his football scholarship.

2007   Enrolls at Passaic County Community College; he returns to UMass that fall and plays his first college game.

2008   Cruz makes the starting lineup in his junior year.

2010   Graduates from UMass, but is not picked in the NFL Draft; Cruz is invited to the New York Giants training camp; he signs with the team in August.

2012   Daughter Kennedy is born on January 9; the Giants win the Super Bowl; Cruz visits the family of murdered Newtown, Connecticut, student Jack Pinto and honors the boy during a game.

2013   Cruz signs a new five-year, $43 million contract with the New York Giants.

CAREER STATISTICS

Year	Team	Games Played	Receptions	Yards	Touchdowns	Fumbles
2010	New York Giants	3	0	0	0	0
2011	New York Giants	16	82	1536	9	1
2012	New York Giants	16	86	1092	10	0

FIND OUT MORE

Books
Cruz, Victor. *Out of the Blue,* Young Reader's Edition. New York: Celebra Children's Books, 2013.

Works Consulted
Cruz, Victor. *Out of the Blue.* New York: New American Library, 2012.

Eisen, Michael. "Victor Cruz: A Success Story." Giants. com, March 20, 2012. http://www.giants.com/ news-and-blogs/article-1/Victor-Cruz-A-success- story/4b0e9c70-d7bb-44b6-8eba-1c401bfc254b

Glauber, Bob. "Victor Cruz Honors Sandy Hook Victim Jack Pinto, 6, Who Idolized Giants Receiver." *Newsday,* December 16, 2012. http://www.newsday.com/ sports/columnists/bob-glauber/victor-cruz-honors- sandy-hook-victim-jack-pinto-6-who-idolized-giants- receiver-1.4340705

Nichols, Rachel. "The Esquire/ESPN *E:60* Little-Big Story of the Week: Victor Cruz and the Great Redemption (with Salsa)." *Esquire,* September 18, 2012. http://www.esquire.com/blogs/culture/victor-cruz- rachel-nichols-12824002

FIND OUT MORE

Pennington, Bill. "Catching On After a Last Chance." *The New York Times,* February 4, 2012. http://www.nytimes.com/2012/02/05/sports/football/giants-victor-cruz-defied-odds-at-umass.html?pagewanted=all&_r=0

Vacchiano, Ralph. "Coughlin 'Incredibly Proud' of Victor Cruz." *Daily News,* December 19, 2012. http://www.nydailynews.com/blogs/giants/2012/12/coughlin-incredibly-proud-of-victor-cruz

On the Internet

New York Giants: "Kids Zone" http://www.giants.com/fan-zone/kids-zone.html

NFL.com: "Victor Cruz" http://www.nfl.com/player/victorcruz/2507855/profile

UMass Athletics: "Victor Cruz" http://www.umassathletics.com/sports/m-footbl/mtt/cruz_victor00.html

GLOSSARY

center (SEN-tuhr)—In football, the player who gives the ball to the quarterback to start a play.

community college (kah-MYOO-ni-tee KOL-ihj)—A local two-year college.

conference (KON-fur-uhnss)—A group of school or professional athletic teams that play against each other regularly.

draft (DRAFT)—An event in which professional teams choose new players.

playoffs (PLEY-offs)—In sports, the games that determine who will go on to play in the championships.

professional (pruh-FESH-uh-nuhl)—Someone who is paid to do something, often something that others do for fun, like football.

receiver (rih-SEE-vuhr)—In football, a player who catches passes.

reception (rih-SEP-shuhn)—A pass that is caught.

running back (RUHN-ing BAK)—In football, a player who carries the ball.

salsa (SAHL-suh)—A type of Latin American music, or the ballroom dance that is performed with salsa music.

scholarship (SKOL-uhr-ship)—Money given to a student to attend a school.

INDEX